Victims
of BULLIES

Domestic Violence and Children
by Timothy White, Sr.

Victims of Bullies © 2016 by Timothy White, Sr.

For information contact:
info@uptownmediaventures.com

Book and Cover design by Tim White Publishing

ISBN: 978-1-68121-109-1

10 9 8 7 6 5 4 3 2 1

Table of Contents

Introduction

In this the third book in the series of writings in which we talk about domestic and other violence, we will focus on bullying. The primary emphasis will be on children, and how bullying and domestic violence affects them.

Lately the media is filled with stories about bullying and children and how it's become seemingly more violent over the years towards them.

The surprise is that bullying is not always coming from other children.

Bullying is a condition and mindset that as human beings we see or have (*it seems*) participated in it, for as long as human beings have existed.

There are many types of bullies and they come from all walks of life.

What are we to do when confronted by a bully, and where do we go for help when the bully is someone we know?

Some of the very people that should protect our children can be found guilty of harming them. This book has been written to help us better understand bullying, and domestic violence, and what we can do to solve them, as well as how they are very similar in nature.

What we know about bullies, and bullying means nothing if we do nothing to confront it or erase it.

What makes someone a bully, where does it come from, and are bullies almost always men as many of us have been taught to believe?

What makes someone a good candidate and victim for bullying? Bullies have a history and it is no mystery.

Bullying can be traced back to a point of origin. One of the major reasons we do not see its cause, is that we are willfully distracted by technology and our fast pace lifestyles that it has been ignored until recent events that are now filling the headlines in media across the country.

Bullying and domestic violence has become like a slow cancer that is ravishing the consciousness of the country, and unless it is dealt with at its source, it will continue to grow and eventually claim the lives of those it inflicts. All of us see and hear about bullying. But what good is that, if nothing is done to change things?

Chapter 1
Collateral Damage

When it comes to domestic violence how does it affect the children who are unfortunately caught in its crossfire? Children become victims as well, and sometimes even become violent themselves as a result.

Who cares about the children, or what violence in the home does to them, are they a consideration at all? No. They are often used as pawns of the relationship to pit one parent against the other, and forced to choose sides. Whichever side they choose will not be the best side.

Children most often choose their mothers because of nurturing and because they usually spend more time at home with mom than they do the father.

Children are seen or supposed to be unintended victims, but more times than not they are simply ignored by the feuding grown-ups.

Collateral damage, is seen as unimportant when it comes to what arguing parents want, the children are not a consideration when violence erupts. Is this unintentional?

Let's look at a few things that take place when

children see, or get caught up in the web of domestic violence.

When it comes to domestic violence, children have not developed strong filters and proper discernment, so it's not uncommon for them to think that the unrest is something they have caused, and so they begin to blame themselves or in some cases harm themselves, believing that doing so would end the violence.

Some other effects are, some children because they are exposed to violence in the home begin to think it's okay to be violent towards others, or even to accept violence against themselves as a way of being loved.

Children living in homes where domestic violence regularly occurs, are more likely to become depressed, have anxiety issues, and even develop poor school performance. Behavior issues, trouble going to sleep, and chronic health problems often occur in these children, and they seek to be away from home as much as possible.

When we see these effects, we dismiss them or label them as something other than being in a violent and confrontational environment.

Sometimes, in order to make their point clear, an abusive spouse will also threaten to do harm to children in the relationship, and some have done so without hesitation.

Domestic violence has side effects that often claim our children. Here's a few more examples to consider.

The moment some children become old enough to use drugs or alcohol *(some preteens have also done so)* they will turn to them, and sex, as a way to cope with the situation they found themselves in.

SUICIDE. Teen girls who witness abuse at home, attempt suicide more often than teen boys.

Sadly, some children who witness one parent hurting or threatening the other, are more likely to get in an abusive relationship themselves when they grow up, and some becoming either a victim or abusers.

How many children witness the abuse of their mothers? The number at the time of this writing is one in three.

It's said that 3-4 million children between the ages of 3-17 are at risk of exposure to domestic violence each year, and that 95% of domestic violence cases involve women being victimized by male partners.

One of the most damaging things to occur with children is, for them to become the witness of domestic violence firsthand.

This means, SEEING incidences of physical/and or sexual abuse. It could mean HEARING threats made or brawling noises from another room. The children may also OBSERVE the aftermath of physical abuse such as blood, bruises, tears, or torn clothing.

The children become AWARE of the tension in the home as it comes closer to the time when the abuser should be on their way home.

Children in abusive relationships become afterthoughts, and not priorities.

They only become important or relevant once someone is hurt or killed, and it is then that onlookers become reactive when they should have been proactive.

There are no do overs, or sorry that can change what has been planted in the minds and lives of these children.

Children who grow up in an abusive home are expected to keep this as a family secret, and that it's no one business what goes on in their home.

Some children from abusive homes are good actors, and they can put on a great show to the outside world that things are fine. Their families are chaotic and crazy.

These same children may also become angry and distant from their siblings or their mother, even blaming her and them for causing the abuse.

Remember what was said earlier, domestic violence effects are not always physical. When it comes to children it can be what they have SEEN or HEARD take place.

So, what if any are the long-term effects on children who come from homes of domestic violence? We have discussed some short-term effects.

Whether or not children are physically abused, they often suffer emotionally and psychologically from the trauma of living in homes where their father abuses their mother.

Children whose mothers are abused are selfishly denied the right to a happy life that fosters good mental and physical development with their children.

Children who grow up seeing their mothers being abused by their father, grow up with a role model that suggest relationships in which one person uses intimidation and violence over another person to get their way is acceptable.

As human beings, but the children in particular, have a natural tendency to identify with power and strength, so, it's not uncommon to ally themselves with the abuser, and lose respect for their seemingly weak mother. This is not always done openly but is largely a mental alliance.

The abusers typically play into this thinking by putting the mother down in front of her children, and telling them that their mother is "crazy", "stupid" or some other vile thing and that they do not have to listen to her.

Seeing their mothers treated with enormous disrespect, teaches children that they can disrespect their mother, as well as other women in the manner their father does.

Children who are raised in abusive homes LEARN THAT VIOLENCE IS AN EFFECTIVE WAY to resolve conflicts and problems.

Children when becoming adults may duplicate the violence they witnessed as children in their teen and adult relationships and even applying this violence to their parenting experiences.

Boys who witness their mothers' abuse are more likely to batter their female partners as adults, than boys raised in homes where there is no such violence.

For girls, preteen and adolescent, witnessing violence may result in the belief that threats and violence are a normal part of their relationship.

Children from violent homes have higher risks of alcohol and drug abuse, post-traumatic stress disorder, and juvenile delinquency.

Witnessing domestic violence ranks high and is said to be one of the best predictors of juvenile delinquency and adult crime. It's also been said to be the number one reason children run away from home.

Collateral damage. What is the cost and the value placed on our children in the home?

Where there are no children it's easy to think in terms of what the individual wants or needs might be. But the moment there are children in the home the focus must shift as we are now dealing with multiple lives.

There's no excuse for violence in the home. If there is violence, one must ask why, as well as what does it stem from, what is its origin, and can it be resolved without violence?

Collateral damage should not take place as an afterthought. It must be examined the moment other lives are involved in a relationship. Children are not pawns, or tools that should be used by adults to get what they want. The damage done can take a lifetime to overcome if it is overcome at all.

NOTES:

Chapter 2
Innocence Corrupted

Adults seldom take time to think about the effects of what they do, or what affect it could possibly have on the innocence of children. As adults we tend to focus on what's in our own best interest and not consider anyone else.

Technology increasingly has made it more difficult to be the parents we should be. Social media has replaced quality time with our children.

The cell phone has become the new parents, Instagram, Facebook, Twitter, and Snap chat, these and other media outlets have replaced the need for parental involvement in the mental wellbeing of children.

Instead of bringing families together they distance them with the justification that this makes it easy to reach out in an emergency.

Children no longer have a dependence on their parents to give them social advice, or encouragement, this has been replaced by the internet, where they can now get insight, and advice from literally hundreds and thousands of people.

So, how is innocence corrupted? It's done through several channels, two of which we are very familiar with.

OVEREXPOSURE and LIFESTYLE.

Some of the most declared statements from the mouth of adults have been, "Times have changed", and things are different now", and "I want to give my child what my parents never gave me".

Parenting requires protective skills. It's not allowing certain things to be part of a child's upbringing.

Does this mean a child should be raised in a box, or in isolation? Absolutely not. Some parents have tried this, only to find rebellion quickly developed and the problem became greater.

Children need, and require balance, and proper physical and mental nourishment to help them grow and make wise and proper decisions.

The danger comes when they are exposed and overexposed to situations their little minds don't fully understand.

Children are mental babies, works in progress, innocent clean slates waiting to be written on.

Children today more than ever are being exposed to things and lifestyles that have become harmful to their growth.

Societies are falling because of overexposure and laziness, as culturally we have now given way to seeking pleasure not parenting.

The corruption of innocence begins when we allow children to raise themselves, to take on roles of adults without understanding the responsibilities that is associated with it, or the consequences for doing so, theirs or ours.

A child's innocence is corrupted for example when they are exposed to drinking, drunkenness, and drug use in the home.

Those who use alcohol often use it as their excuse for violence, blaming the drink and not the drinker as the reason for abuse as a way of shifting responsibility away from them for their actions.

50 percent of sexual assaults against women and children is attributed to alcohol consumption

It's been said that researchers investigating the role of alcohol abuse determined it was both a cause of abuse and a consequence of child abuse. This by no means suggest that this is always the case, but it is often a contributing factor with children putting them at a greater risk.

Studies on alcohol has found that childhood abuse and neglect frequently are associated with adult alcohol problems.

Most individuals turn to alcohol as a coping mechanism, to help them through situations known only to them. Again, I must remind you that children are the forgotten people in this picture.

Almost everywhere we turn we see that alcohol is used as a way of socializing, relaxing or coping with life's stresses. You can't find many shows on TV that do not promote drinking and commercials that sell, sell, sell, or promote alcohol.

Research has found there is a link between the use of alcohol and personal violence (*like suicide*), interpersonal violence (*that is domestic abuse, rape, homicide*) and even group violence (*such as unruliness and riotous acts at sporting events*).

When we bring a child into this type of environment, we expose them to an act or action that is advertised as acceptable, even when it turns abusive and violent.

Children being impressionable, see and accept this behavior as being normal and acceptable with many growing to imitate it.

Alcohol is the triggering stimulus to a much deeper problem and unresolved issues.

Adults, and now many children, use alcohol as their way to cope with what they call stress, and they, the children, have become rebellious, and become violent themselves, due to overexposure to this type of lifestyle.

Consider the following also as it comes to children. It's not only the man that can be abusive, women can be just as abusive also.

Children coming from homes that have a history of drinking and drug abuse are more likely to suffer from physical, emotional, and sexual abuse.

Drinking parents cannot protect their children from any abuse that they might be directed at them, and they might very well be the cause of that abuse.

Many women being battered will often take out their anger on their children for the alcohol abuse, and domestic abuse inflicted on them by a partner, and instead of fighting back or seeking outside help their children make easy targets, sadly these children see their mothers as safe. This type of abuse of children coming from frustrated women is said to be as high as eighty percent.

The aftereffects of this innocence being corrupted is that many of these children often grow to have their own drug and alcohol problems, as they attempt to cope with the pains of the abuse they have suffered.

Children can be exposed to all the positive teaching in the world, but this does not mean they will follow that teaching, but the odds are greater in their favor, the more they have positive influences in their lives.

There are three types of exposure to consider here...

1. Underexposure
2. Overexposure, and
3. Proper exposure

As we have said earlier in this chapter, parenting requires balance, which also includes regular and continuous involvement in a child's life, not this new absentee parenting because of work.

Children should not be sheltered from experiencing certain aspects of life and some of its disappointments, but they should not become victims of abuse and violence in doing so in this learning process.

Now let's take a look at the three types of exposures we mentioned.

Underexposure

Underexposed is to have a fear for children to learn or experience certain aspects of life that is not always positive or healthy, and it is to lack clarity. It's guided by fear, and fear can be destructive, and dangerous if there is no clarity.

Underexposed is not seeing things clearly or what could take place because of inaction or a willing blindness.

Let's be honest, innocence is not corrupted by accident, it's most often done by those who are selfish and thinking only of themselves and not others, particularly, children.

Underexposed does not mean unaware but simply not doing what is required to act appropriate given particular situations.

Many parents are guilty of underexposure with their children, another word for this is, NEGLECT.

Child abuse is also neglecting parental responsibilities and proper care of a child.

Protecting our children does not mean keeping knowledge from them that can help them as they grow and explore the world they are now part of.

Education should be done on the child's level of understanding. As adults and parents, we have a moral responsibility to our children to educate as well as protect them.

"Personal Safety", physical, and mental safety should be a first, not last consideration where our children are concerned.

Innocence is often short lived, and once it is removed, or corrupted it's something that cannot be repaired or restored, but it can be adjusted with knowledge and application.

Overexposure

Overexposure is giving too much, too soon, to overdo, to push out before time. This is where many of us as adults fail, it's not allowing a child, to be a child.

Example, when it concerns other siblings, particularly younger brothers and sisters, some parents push the older children to become responsible for caring for, and parenting their siblings, in effect kids raising kids. Yes, there is a certain amount of responsibility that goes with being an older child, but remember they are still only children.

A child is not a parent and should not be made to act like one (*which is impossible since they do not have the mentality to do so*). Children left along to their own devises find themselves doing, acting out, and saying things that are inappropriate. Siblings as we will detail in another chapter can also become some of the first bullies a child knows.

Children are not tiny adults no matter how much the attempt to make them so. Children are still in the developmental stage of life and should not be forced to take on responsibilities they are not ready for.

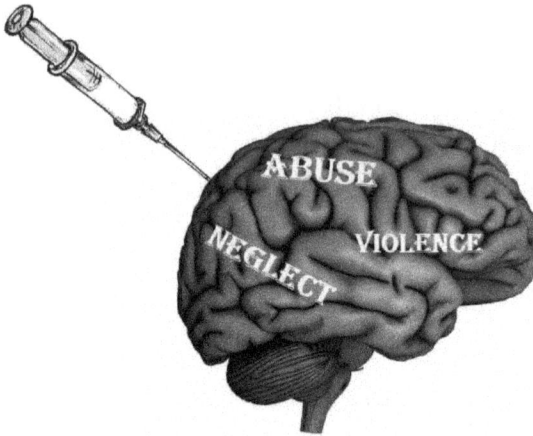

Our children are having their innocence being corrupted by mental injections of neglect thinking, abusive behavior and violence directly injected into their brains (*consciousness*).

The cure for this is simple although ignored by many.

We have now seen the danger of giving too much too soon, by overexposure, and we see the danger of underexposure (*giving too little to help*). The balance comes by way of proper exposure.

Proper Exposure

Proper exposure. Doing what's right not always what's convenient. This means not only taking time to teach, but to listen as well. It's understanding that children are people too, and it's our responsibility to discipline, guide, and educate them, morally, emotionally, and spiritually.

It's being careful not to poison their minds, neglect or abuse them. Proper exposure means being sensitive to their needs and willing to learn from them also.

Far too many adults believe they are above learning, and especially from a young person or child, and this is a mental poison.

Poison's impact is never forgotten even when healing has taken place. We never forget what poison can do, and so we must be mindful that we can become poison to our children that we boast we love if we are not careful.

Our country is now filled with distractions and denial. We question why so many people do the things they do, and that we did not see the signs, or that these people were good people before they did what they did.

Yes, we want to know why, but we don't want the answer to be found lying at our doorsteps.

Innocence is corrupted on the most basic of levels. It's done gradually but continuously, and many, if not all of us can share in the blame.

NOTES:

Chapter 3
Bullies

How do we define bully? We hear about them and see them all the time in all aspects of media. Children are using and developing various campaigns to address bullying much in the same way that Nancy Reagan did on September 14, 1986 with the "Just say No" campaign in an effort to raise drug abuse awareness.

Awareness was only the first step as it let the country know how dangerous and how much damage drug use was doing to the individual as well as the country.

But awareness needs to be coupled with prevention if there is going to be any measurable success.

Today, in 2017 there is another war being waged and one of the new enemies is bullying, and many organizations are beginning to speak out about bullying, but what do we know about bullying?

Sadly, we even have a president who uses bully tactics in an attempt to get what he wants; using what has been called "his Bully Pulpit."

The greatest danger of bullying unfortunately is coming from the top (White House) down to the average lives and homes.

What can be done about bullying? In order for us to do something about it we must first know something about bullying and bullies.

A bully is defined as a cruel and brutal person, a bossy individual, a domineering person, a hired thug, insulting, hostile, threatening and

aggressive. A bully is a person who forces another to do something by intimidation or violence.

This is by no means a complete definition of bully, but it paints a picture that is very clear to see.

With this in mind we must also point out that there are many types of bullies in the world, and the truth is we have focused on one in particular when all bullies need to be addressed.

When it comes to the truth, it can be very offensive to those who are found guilty of violating it. As we look at bullying and our children, we must also look at the different levels of bullies as well and it might come as a surprise to some readers who these bullies are.

Let's also be clear in this, bullies are not always male. There are many women who have become bullies also, and more recently they have been making the news and being seen for who they are.

As unlikely this pairing might appear, **domestic violence and bullying walk hand in hand**, they are very much related one to the other, and they are a destructive combination.

When we think or speak of domestic violence it is almost exclusively looked at as violence in the home and against a partner in a relationship.

Domestic violence reach is far beyond the home setting as we will show here.

Domestic violence is physical, emotional,

or sexual abuse directed towards a partner, spouse, or other member of a household.

When it comes to domestic violence we tend to place it in a separate category than bullying, when they are in fact closely associated with one another as they both can bring about physical and emotional harm to the one it is inflicted on, and in this book we are focused on children.

Bullies are not born being so, it's LEARNED BEHAVIOR, adopted by the individual and adapted to their choices in life. Something takes place in the life of an individual that points them in that direction.

What that might be depends on a number of things as we will consider.

As we have already said, some children being raised in a home where there is domestic violence will most often lean in the direction of violence themselves and some will later become bully's as a result.

Bullying is a result stemming from some previous negative cause.

As mentioned, there are many types of bully's and we will discuss a number of them, and it might offend some readers when we see who can and has bullied.

As much as we would like to say there are only

certain individuals that bully people, the truth is, many of us have been guilty of or continues to bully others as well.

Here is a short list of people who are potential bullies.

I) Dad
II) Mom
III) Siblings
IV) Teachers
V) Students
VI) Coaches
VII) Adults/Police/ Judges/Attorney's
VIII) Bosses
IX) Social Media /Internet

If this is true, who can we trust or depend on not to bully? I know it might seem very scary to know anyone can be subject to wrong actions, but once we know this, it also becomes easier for us to know what we should look for, and how to respond properly when we see it.

Let's briefly look at each of the types we have numbered here to see if they can qualify for domestic violence or bullying.

I) **Dad**

In order for us to get a clear picture of domestic and other violence it's wise to begin in the home. We will take a look at the family as being one that includes dad.

In the chapter "Didn't ask to be here" it's important to know that the children in a relationship did not create themselves but were the result of a chosen action between the parents.

I would like to say before we continue, that discipline is different than abuse, as one, discipline is done from love, and the other, abuse, is done from anger.

I was taught that the man's part in the home was to be a guide to teaching and leading the family, and being the spiritual guide and voice of reason, and an example for the wife and children.

Dads are not seen in the same light today, as many of them feel stressed that they have to work harder, and have less to show for it, and that they have very little free time to themselves or with their friends.

Men tend to bottle up their feelings because this is what they have been told a man does. A man does not express himself like a woman, or he is considered soft, a push over, and weak.

Some men attempt to be good fathers as they

have gone through and come home from wars carrying the scars and mental wounds of war.

But inside are pinned up feelings and aggression, stress, and other feelings that eat at him. So, many men turn to drugs and alcohol to cope, and in doing so put a strain on the family relationship, and ultimately turn violent emotionally, physically and sexually in an effort to control their environment when outside help is needed.

Childhood baggage, or harmful situations and failed relationships that occurred in the past yet unresolved influence attitudes and actions.

Bear in mind also those **dads who are not biological parents, who don't feel they should be responsible for someone else mistake** (child), and so treat these children in the relationship with disrespect often bullying them, or abusing them physically.

Being a father does not mean he will be a responsible parent, and when tempers flare between couples they can become verbally abusive, and can lead to physical abuse as well.

Children should never become the recipients of anger, and disagreements among adults.

Men are taught that they are King of the castle, and that their word is law in the home, and they are never to be challenged or questioned. Having this mentality often brings with it danger.

It's **the Alpha Male Syndrome**, "I'm the leader of the pack", "the head", "no one is better than me", "I'm the boss", and like a marathon race this belief is passed on from one generation to the next, and can have deadly consequences.

This mental and toxic poison has not only damaged homes, but countless lives throughout the country.

Dads (men) are subject to the same mindset they developed as children and it could be abuse, violence, or even drugs that triggers an outburst or violence (*You can read more on this in my book In the Ring with heels on*).

Children on the receiving end of this type of anger, question themselves as to what they might have done. And the abusers will blame the child for whatever inappropriate behavior that follows.

Instead of communicating, many Dads threaten or carry out acts of violence to prove they mean what they say.

It should also be said that just because a dad is not in the home does not mean he doesn't have influence in it. Being outside the home can be more dangerous than inside, as the bullying is often more focused on the child during times of visitations.

This becomes the time to as we have already spoken, to inject the PARENTAL POISON into the mind of a child.

II) **Mom**

Is it possible for mom's to also be bullies? The answer is yes. How can that be so, she is the caregiver and the parent thought to be the one that gives unconditional love to their children. As we have stated, domestic violence is not limited to men only, and there are many incidences of women who are also violent towards their partners, as well as their children.

What would make a woman want to harm her children? There are countless reasons for that, some of which we give in the book (*She's the Boss, domestic violence against men*).

There are women, who like men, have been hurt, maybe at home, or in a relationship and unfortunately seek to hurt others or themselves as their way of coping with that pain. Some women like men, turn to alcohol, drugs and sex to find what they call peace for a short period of time.

Unfortunately some of this abuse is directed at children when there is a divorce involved (particularly if the child looks like the other parent), often being told "you're no good just like your father", "he was nothing and so are you", and " I hate looking at you".

It was stated that alcohol and drugs can play a major part in mothers becoming bullies as they become the single parent of the household, believing they now have to rule with an iron fist, and become threatening to their children to get compliance.

Children have no real defense against abusive parents, and they begin to internalize their struggles and often feelings of inferiority and neglect.

Lately we are hearing more about children that suffered abuse at the hand of their parents doing the unthinkable, they killed their parents citing this was the only way for them to become free of their abuse. A story such as the Menendez Brothers, Lyle and Eric's murder case, where they say they were physically and sexually abused as young children, who as adults murdered their parents. Their story being only a small part and beginning of verbal abuse that came from other sources as well.

III) **Siblings**

Many children suffer from bullying that begins at home where there are other siblings present. Much of the bullying that begins at home is transferred and transitions outside the home to many other places and individuals.

Children don't think about how hurtful they can be towards other siblings often mimicking what their parents say or do in taunts and insults.

Many of the first acts of bullying starts in the home. Older children feel entitled to certain things because they are older and will pick on younger children to hurt their feelings or see them cry.

"You're not my brother/sister", "you were an accident", "nobody likes you".

For a sibling to hit, kick, punch or yell at a brother or sister is considered or seen as acceptable, and it's not a hidden behavior because that's what children do. But, the seeds of abuse and violence is being planted in their consciousness and rooted in their subconscious as the most effective way to control others, and to make that sibling feel they are less valuable and unimportant when compared to them.

Bullying is, if uncorrected a show of power and

force that if ignored as a minor problem that children grow away from, but many don't, and ultimately poisons behavior. History is telling us a very violent story.

Bullying is forced compliance using threats, intimidation, and even violence to assure that what is demanded is done.

IV) Teachers

What happens in the home does not remain in the home, there is a carryover into other aspects of a child's life as they grow. The problem of abuse, verbal or otherwise, is carried with a child long after they leave the home as children, and some even into adulthood.

Can teachers be bullies, and contribute to the internal conflict and harm of a child? The answer is yes. How often do we hear adults say they were influenced by their teachers? Teachers are educators, and some of them have used less than kind words to convey their message to the young ears of the classroom.

There have been teachers who have abused students physically, emotionally as well as sexually and leaving unseen scars, some lasting a lifetime.

As parents we entrust our children to an

educational system for 6 hours and more a day. This book is not about finger pointing but bringing awareness to issues that are often ignored or pacified and not properly dealt with.

Knowing a problem exist does not solve it, and throwing money at it does not clear these issues up or make them go away.

To solve any problem, we must trace them back to the source and work forward from there.

All human beings are flawed individuals carrying their past as life baggage, positive and negative.

Low Self-esteem

Those who bully suffer from low self-esteem. This does not mean they are unintelligent or have a low IQ. In fact, you will find the opposite is often true. Bullies are usually very intelligent people, and they can be very manipulating and Charismatic.

The individuals that make up our lives are not known for being ignorant, but they have become forceful, threatening, and intimidating to achieve what they want from you.

Recently the light has shown vigorously on those who bully, as it is now shining in a national spotlight, and no longer seen as a local or individual problem.

Domestic violence is one of the fuels of abuse, and bullying, and is a contributing factor to the decay of our nation.

V) **Students**
Leaving the home does not mean leaving domestic violence or bullying behind. This disrespect for others can be found everywhere we go.

Children intimidating other children has become a new way of life found in schools and classrooms around the country.

Children as young as 5-8 years of age are being abused and bullied. This abuse reaches from daycare to College. The victimization of children is one of the methods to control them, by enslaving their minds from an early age.

Bullies' tend to see themselves as weak and do things to appear to be strong by causing hurt to another as a demonstration of power and strength.

Unfortunately, there are bullies all around us in every walk of life from politicians to police, to doctors and dentist, from the wealthy to the poor you can find them.

Bullies thrive on fear, they love having people afraid of them, or what they can do

Children have not developed fully mentally as therefore subject to greater influence when it concerns bullying and intimidation.

When I was a child the bullies were those who went around threatening to beat you up if you did not give them what they wanted or did what they said.

Bullying is not new, it changes from one generation to the next, but in doing so, it's become more violent and destructive, due in part to technology as we will speak more to later in this chapter.

As children we seek to "belong", to be a family, it's in our DNA, and because of this, many children begin to organize into groups.

These groups can be gangs, they can be Sororities, or Fraternities, where people can find those who share their beliefs.

But in order to qualify for these "groups" it's necessary to pass their test. Many children are bullied into joining these groups by others, and sometimes parents because they were a part of a particular group themselves.

Children bullying other children is not seen as divisive until harm results. Bullying is normal until someone is hurt, or dies.

When a child bully's, hit, kick, punch, or throws something at another child this is violence not normal.

Violence towards another child or any human being is not cute or laughable, but it's often made excusable by saying "that's what kids do".

VI) Coaches

Win, win, win. Coaches can be bullies and exploit their positions and are generally accepted for doing so.

I know this goes against the grain for many people as we see sports as being as much a part of our lives as the American flag.

But we must take a closer look at what coaching involves.

It's yelling and screaming at players to do better, push harder, and win. It's a hurt the other player competition. It's about having a team spirit to be on top.

Hit them, hurt them, crush them, destroy them. Does this sound like sportsmanship?

Locker room talk with a losing team is not one of "just play a good game" or "you are doing your best".

Coaches can become vial in the pursuit of championships, and will talk down to players, and as we have seen, some are not opposed to striking a player. Are we talking about NFL? No, this takes place around the country to children playing and entering sports even on a junior level.

Coaches have been caught yelling and screaming profanities at children, pushing them, and hitting them, is this coaching or bullying?

Children being exposed to this type of teaching and behavior become confused and many become depressed, and distant, with parents wondering why. The things that happen behind closed doors and unseen by the masses affect the minds of our children and is carried over into their seemingly mysterious actions of distancing themselves, rebellion and even hurting themselves.

Children entering into brutal sports often develop brutal habits, being taught to hit, hurt, and take what you want or have to if you are going to be a winner, and to do anything less is to be considered a loser, a disappointment to the team and shameful.

VII) **Adults/Police/ Judges etc...**

As you notice the progression the abusive mentality and violence goes through a process and for most of us it took place by way of something that happened in the past and triggered by a present or recent incident.

Let's face the truth, even the violence that we deem a mystery once investigated is linked to something that took place in that individuals past.

As adults we tend to bury the ugly side of our childhood beneath other things or activities, rather than admit to what might be causing pain in our relationship with others.

Some adults seek positions of power to prove their self-worth, and some use that power sadly to get even with others who have caused them harm, and thereby becoming bullies themselves.

Past pains don't go away just because we become adults, they need to be addressed or they will again rear their heads, and the results can be domestic abuse, violence and bullying.

Bullying goes across all cultures and into all walks of life.

In the news, and social media, we find some police have become nothing more than bullies with badges, and instead of protecting and serving, many now intimidate and harass, and even becoming gang like in their tactics.

The excuse we give for Police violence is they are under unusual stress due to the jobs they hold, so, does this give them the right to abuse their wives, children or the public?

Judges having a bad day should not go home and take it out on their family or on a defendant. What's in the home will ultimately filter out into the community.

Angry people tend to become bullies

Adults that bully justify their anger and actions as being necessary for the better good. And the easiest victims are the defenseless and the innocent.

VIII) **Bosses**

As parents, those of us who are, we've been given the challenge of being caretakers of another life or lives. And what we are to impart to them is knowledge, and prepare them for the time they will leave home, and enter into the work force or real world.

Many of the bullies spoken of here, some children have not had to face yet, but we need to be aware, and make them aware, that bullies can be found in every aspect of their lives, as well as our own lives.

Remember what we said about a marathon, many

of the things a child is exposed to in the home they will ultimately pass on to others.

It's the responsibility of the parents to teach their children what to be careful of, and what to avoid. But this can only take place if the parents are in the child's life and not just in the home.

IX) Social Media/ Iphones and Internet

Another very clear and present danger is the advent of social media, iphones and the internet.

These things have become the principle teachers of our children and they rely on them for education and truth.

We cannot conclude this chapter on bullying without talking about viral stalking and bullying over the internet.

With Facebook reaching more than 2 billion subscribers it has made it increasingly easy for someone to bully, and remain almost anonymous.

Overall there are no filters on social media, and very few restrictions. You can find foul language, to all out brawls posted for what some see as entertainment.

Parents, for the most part, have no idea what their children are looking at or being exposed to until for some it's too late. Children, are not little adults, and should not be treated as such. They need moral guidance and discipline to help them develop properly.

What does all this show? Acceptance. We have become jaded as a culture, and as a people to become accepting of behavior that is contrary, and that is morally corrupt and violent.

Bullying is now called competing to be the best. But in order to be considered the best it is to be compare to someone or something else that is now seen as less valuable.

All life has value and should never be seen or treated as less. Bullying corrupts the minds, and lives of others. It will not change until we change.

NOTES

Chapter 4
What Did I Do?

When it comes to violence in the home, children unconsciously wonder what it is they might have done to bring it about. They develop emotions of guilt and shame, as they struggle to make sense of the abuse they suffer at the hands of the people they look up to, love and respect.

A child whose mind is yet in the developmental stage, will associate hurt with something they believe they have done, or believe they might have done.

Domestic violence has a trickle-down effect, going from the parents to child, other siblings, and into the community.

Children can become bullies, or victims of bullies, many times because of what takes place in their homes, or allowed to take place in the home.

What did I do, this question is asked mentally and emotionally? It is not asked vocally for fear of being thought challenging the individual who has caused their discomfort. **Words matter and they are the first form of abuse towards others or self**.

Children that are in mental and emotional development (*as all children are*), will do things or imitate things they see done hoping to get a positive response for their action, as a demonstration of love.

Be mindful, that to an abuser they see negative actions as positive, if they get the response they seek. This will become clearer as we go along.

Children are life's crown jewels. They did not ask to be born and should not be treated as mistakes, and hindrances in our lives.

In the home, some children are treated differently, for example, if they are children of previous or another relationship (*Often being called STEPCHILDREN*), and with labels such as half-brother or sister, (*if having different fathers*), or foster children.

This is most frequently done to place a divide between them, and into the consciousness of the other children, that they are not equal to the other children, who are biological to the relationship. Let's be clear, these are divisive labels used to place children on different levels of what some say is love, should something go wrong in the relationship.

Of course, there are some parents that say they

love all these children equally, and there is a percentage that do their best to apply this in the home.

At the same time, there are those who often harbor resentment against these non-biological children, and it festers inside waiting to be released, often occurring in times of stress, depression and anger towards the parent of these children. (*they wanted the relationship, but not the baggage that comes with them and only tolerates the children accordingly*).

It has become easy to also blame children for failing relationships, to fault their upbringing on the now offensive and offending parent. But, little consideration is given to how the actions of adults affect children.

On a personal note, I will share here for the first time in written form how I also was a victim of abuse and violence in the home as a child. This did not take place in the home with my family but in foster care as a child.

My mother became sick with tuberculosis, and she wasn't able to keep the family together during the time of her illness, and we were all placed in various homes for almost a year as she recovered.

Another of my brothers (*younger*), and another

child we did not know at the time was with us, for what I look back on, felt like imprisonment.

I did not know the process of foster care at that time but I'm sure it was not supposed to be what we experienced at the time.

The woman we stayed with, looking back only did it for the money, as it certainly was not because she loved kids.

Even to this day I have very vivid memories of that time and the abuse it included. As a child I did not understand what my mother was enduring, only that our family was torn apart.

The home my brother and I were in was in those days foster care, and the woman (*I will call her Mrs. G*) who was in charge of the home, was not very pleasant, and my memories of her were not joyous to say the least.

As a child I did not understand drinking and what it could do until then, and how it would lead to many abusive incidences, a few I relate here.

It's important to know that a child can overcome many things in life, but make no mistake about it, they don't always forget what they have gone through, but a child, even a very young child, will ask themselves, what did they do that they are being abused and harmed?

I chose to look back and learn from what took place rather than live in anger, and resentment as these are choices we have when any of us experience hurt or physical harm.

One day I recall taking a piece of candy from the dish on the table, and eating it, and was accused of stealing it (*there were no rules and guidelines for us to follow or so I thought*) and I was beat for my action.

I was tied to the door and whipped by my foster mothers' son, as she was a very large woman who was unable or possibly unwilling to do things for herself.

There would be many such beatings taking place during the almost year we spent in Mrs. G's home.

There was another time I was sent to bed hungry for using up ketchup, which she used up while in a drunken state. My brother brought me a slice of bread which I tore into small pieces rolled them up and put them in my pockets and when hungry I placed one at a time in my mouth sticking it to the roof of my mouth and rubbed it with my tongue until it dissolved.

Some might ask, why didn't I tell my mother? I was threatened not to do so, or it would be much worse the next time, this was an act of bullying. In those days it was much easier for a child to comply when adults spoke.

There was another time that I was punished I think it was pure meanness, I was told to clean up the dog's poop (*of which there were two*), from the floor, using only my hands to do so.

As I have already said, she was a very large woman and very lazy about housework, and any other work for that matter.

She would yell out "EMERGENCY" which was the signal to bring the pan for her to pee in, which I had to hold while she did so, and then carry it and empty it.

The times that our mom would visit was always announced in advance, and Mrs. G would have us clean-up for the visits, and she threaten us to not say a word of what took place in the house.

This secret was kept from my mother for months. My mother somehow became very suspicious at how we were acting, and knew something was not right.

Its good for parents to know their children.

There were numerous incidences of untold abuse. Mrs. G was eventually found out by our mom, and the social worker who stopped by unannounced, finding her asleep and drunk in a chair and breast hanging out.

You might be wondering why it seems that so much was happening to me and not my brother and the other child. In large part it was that I was the oldest of us three, and therefore best suited (*this is only my guess*) to make an example of to keep them in line.

Needless to say, there was a certain amount of fear that I lived with, not knowing what might happen next.

I share this not because I want to, or have to, but to let others know that the power to overcome being a victim rest within each of us. It always seems easier to blame ourselves for what others have done, and thinking just maybe it must be our fault, and that this can be the only reason we are being abused.

It must also be said, that childhood experiences have lasting effects on us. I had to decide even as a child the course I would have to choose for myself. We were bullied in foster care. And because of it, inside, if allowed to, were planted the seeds of bullying because of being hurt. **Often when we hurt,**

it can become easy to pass that pain along to others by our actions.

Being a child is not a disease, and it's not a child's fault for adults' personal unhappiness.

As many children do, I asked myself what did I do wrong, and why were these things happening to me?

My innocence was shattered, and it became difficult (*for a while*) to get close to some people or even to allow many adults to get close to me as a child, without fearing I might be abused again.

Many people have asked over the years, how did I get through it? On the top of the list was to not blame myself for what I had no control over. People who have not suffered often say, "you'll be okay", that's easy to say but not easy to do. It's a process that the abused go through, sometimes it might take a few years, sometimes it might take a lifetime to heal, it's different for everyone, but everyone can heal in time, given time.

Do you ever get over these things that happened to you in the past, no, but we can get through them, and this requires help, whether counseling, or spiritual guidance or both?

As a young man (*teenager*) I also gave my life to Christ and believe me, I learned what the true meaning of love is, and I live accordingly to this day.

I have healed in many areas, and continue to heal in others, but many of the scars remain to tell the story. It's vital that we are extremely careful of the things we say, and do with our children, as well as to them.

As adults, many of us don't consider what our actions do, or what affect they will have on our children, or other children as we seek to gratify our own urges, and advancing our own interest.

Children of abuse always ask the question as to what they did to become recipients of abuse, neglect or violence. Ultimately, they blame themselves as they are children believing it has to be something they did, to cause this abuse.

As a child, it's much easier to accept the abuse if you think you did something to bring it about, or that this is a normal part of life.

Abuse should never be thought of as normal, and a child should never ask themselves what did they do to receive abuse or bullying?

NOTES:

Chapter 5
Hell House

Hell house, was the name of a movie, and when you think of the words hell house, it conjures up visions of an evil and dark place, where mysterious and wicked things take place.

Unfortunately, there are children who have been residents of actual hell houses, places of evil and wickedness.

Seldom do we know what goes on behind closed doors unless tragedy strikes, and the media gets word of it.

On the surface things appear to be what we call normal, and wholesome. But we know all things are not what they appear.

For a child, home should be the closest place to paradise on earth. It should be known for its comfort, safety and love.

So, what is it that takes a house from a place of paradise to it becoming a house of horrors and hell?

We have all heard the statement, "if these walls could talk". The wall cannot talk but the secrets that were hidden behind those walls speak through the people who survived, who broke the silence, and released the pain they had been carrying, some for decades.

They understood they were not weak, that they were abused and that it wasn't anything they did to receive the abuse.

Why are children abused? Three reasons:
1) they are easy,
2) they are innocent, and
3) they are vulnerable.

Being brought up under abuse has its own set of challenges for a child, male and female.

Abuse, bullying, and domestic violence is not new and there are many people that suffered it, even famous people that you might not be aware of, I give a few here.

Drew Barrymore says that she suffered unspecified child abuse at the hands of her father, John Barrymore, who struggled with chronic alcohol addiction. Drew was exposed to alcohol and drugs before she reached her teens, and emancipated herself from her parents at the age of 15, after a suicide attempt and drug rehab two years earlier.

Oprah Winfrey while taping a show in 1986 revealed to her audience that she was raped by a family member when she was just 9 years old. Since then she's tried to use her own experience to help other victims.

Marilyn Monroe was one of the first celebrities to openly discuss being abused as a child. She lived in a series of foster homes and eventually married at 16, she said, simply to avoid a another foster placement.

Queen Latifah says that she was sexually abused as a child, but did not name her abuser. "He violated me," she said.

I never told anybody...I was a kid, and I had no power or control over the situation. I really wish I'd had the strength and the knowledge to say something sooner."

Bill Clinton. His stepfather Roger Clinton was an alcoholic who physically abused the future 42nd president of the United States. Clinton said that as a child he never spoke out about the abuse. Not unusual as most children were afraid of what might happen to them if they told someone.

Tyler Perry. The prolific writer/ director told Oprah that his father physically abused him, and that he also experienced sexual abuse from other adults in his life.

Chevy Chase. The famed comedian of Saturday Night Live wrote in his autobiography that his mother and his stepfather would lock him in a closet for hours and slap his face before releasing him.

Eleanor   Roosevelt Historians have revealed that the former first lady was abused as a child, but she never spoke about it in public. Even as she was described she was said to be homely and an unattractive woman

Rosie Perez The actress has written about being abused as a child, by her schizophrenic mother and by the nuns at the group home where she was placed in foster care at age 3.

Tavis Smiley The nationally syndicated radio talk show host wrote in his autobiography about being abused by his stepfather, the details of which are not openly discussed. Dealing with abuse is an ongoing process.

Mary J. Blige says that she was sexually abused as a child, and that this has inspired some of her lyrics, which speak about the importance of rising above terrible experiences. She, like others have shown the past cannot hold you down, or hold you back

.

Robert Blake. Child star (member of Little Rascals Our Gang series as Micky), TV star (starred in the show Baretta), and the star in the movie In Cold Blood. He said that as a child he was abused physically, sexually, and mentally. He would later turn to drugs and alcohol as a coping tool. He would be arrested and later convicted of killing his wife.

Famous people were once children also, and they were not always famous, nor did any of them think that one day they might be. They had to deal with abuse, sexual, mental, and physical in their personal hell houses.

Sadly, not every story of abuse is a success story such as in the case of Mr. Blake, I only gave one here, but they are numerous.

Domestic violence, and abuse is that dirty little secret hidden behind locked doors.

It's clearly possible to go from being a victim to being victorious, it's a choice everyone has to make and can make with help, emotionally or spiritually, what seems to be impossible becomes possible, and once it is believed it can be achieved.

As we have already said the easiest prey and victims for abuse and violent behavior are children. We will never know what goes on in the home if we never take time to get involved.

There are countless individuals who have suffered violence and abuse, movie and TV stars as well as what we call everyday people.

Some people choose to see themselves as victims only, whereas others see themselves as victorious. The path they choose is theirs and theirs alone. Coming from a house of hell does not mean that hell has to become a practiced lifestyle.

We all live with scars. A scar is a wound that has healed but left a reminder of what you have gone or suffered through.

Each of us has the power to overcome adversity, but that's a personal choice we have to make. It's a challenge to change. A challenge to break the cycle of abuse or to perpetuate it.

It's a choice each of us has to make, to continue to believe we are always going to be a victim, or we are going to stand up and become victorious.

Hell house, begins with the mental and emotional house we build, and ends with taking up a physical residence by conscious and negative actions.

Our children should never see home as less than paradise or a place of safety from hurt, harm or danger.

NOTES:

Chapter 6
Didn't Ask To Be Here

There are two schools of thought when it comes to this statement and we will take a look at both of them.

A child might say, and many have done so, "I didn't ask to be here". What exactly is the "here" they refer to? Some of them are saying they did not ask to be here, meaning born into this world.

Most children, and young people uttering these words are doing so out of defiance, anger or rebellion, but the root cause of the words is pain. What type of pain depends on the child and the experience connected to it.

Usually when a child utters these words they are feeling alone, isolated or threatened.

There are at least two ways of expressing this statement, **1)** it's done lashing out yelling or screaming in despair and **2)** it's done in tones not heard by anyone other than themselves, a quiet frustration with an undertone that could lead to them hurting themselves, and feelings they may have shared with someone close to them or possibly hurting themselves.

Children, have not emotionally matured enough to deal with issues greater than their personal experiences or understanding on specific levels.

It's dangerous to force a child to grow up to soon, making them responsible for taking care of younger siblings, to live their young lives not having, or enjoying a childhood.

Children are not miniature parents, and should not be expected to be such. Many children are living with these internal scars.

Being rich or famous does not exclude a child from carrying these internal scars.

The famous Michael Jackson said, he and his siblings did not have what is called a normal childhood, but was forced to become a singing group.

Yes, they became famous, world known, and rich, but Michael said he missed having a childhood, and many of his songs reflected that (*such as give me back my childhood*).

Michael said they even suffered emotional and physical abuse, as their father (Joe) would beat them if they missed steps during rehearsals.

They were forced at times to rehearse all night, even on school days until they got things right as their father demanded.

All of the Jackson children had stories of abuse they endured by the hand of their father as he pushed them to become what he wanted them to be. This is seen time and time again as parents seek to live their lives or fantasies through their children.

The second view of I didn't ask to be here is that of environment. A child says this when they are uncomfortable with a situation they might be in.

This does not mean where they live is negative, but that they are in opposition to being there personally.

This is what I felt in foster care. I did not want to be separated from my family but neither I or the other members of my family had a choice in the matter.

Children who are non-biological to the home they live in, often feel this way as they don't always feel they are wanted or welcomed in a relationship that is not blood related. It's a sense of not belonging or being on the outside.

Children of domestic violence, and bullying see themselves as being "in the way", or unwanted, especially when there are other children older than them, who push them around, and tell them in threatening words what to do, or how they would harm them if they did not do as they were told.

The danger here is one I have stated before, it's when adults say, "they are children" and "that's just what kids do". And if the child seeks help from the adult they are often told, "STOP BEING SUCH A BABY" or worse.

Some children being tired of being bullied and not being taken seriously run away from home if they can. It would be better to be gone, to leave, and take their chances on the street than continue to live in a home filled with domestic violence and bullying they say, particularly when they are victims.

Many adults have missed the signs of loneliness, fear, and depression in children because they don't believe it's serious enough to give it attention.

When a child begins to isolate themselves from family and friends, it's an indicator that something is not right, and needs to be investigated not ignored.

Children who are bullied want to get away from everything and everyone they believe can hurt them, even family.

Bullies don't care how others feel

As a child going through foster care, I was told

by our foster care provider on many occasions that she did not want us there, that she did not care about us, and she couldn't wait for us to leave.

As children we were not given a choice of where we would be, and no one could foresee what would take place.

Today we are discovering the violence being done to our children by way of camera's being located in homes and videos clearly showing the abuse children have secretly endured, some for years.

We are told that resources are thin, and there aren't enough people to investigate what is going on behind closed doors.

Let's also remember these children did not ask to be put into these situations, and it's not their fault the things that take place, but it's ours for allowing them to continue to take place by non-action, and deliberate denial.

Had my mother not been paying attention to the warning signs and knowing her child and my brother, and had she not notice how my words and actions did not match, chances are the abuse would have continued much longer. But because she knew her children, her action led to making a surprised visit and the truth being exposed.

Children need our help, not our sympathy.

They need our love, not lies. Not one child in this world asked to be here, but they are here and it's our responsibility to nurture and care for them as they go through life.

Not one child asked to be here, but that's not what's important, what is important is how we are going to treat them now that they are here.

NOTES:

Chapter 7
"I Wish I Was Dead"

How sad it is that a child would ever utter these words. But it's almost commonplace to hear some child express them, write them, or share them with close friends, and even now post their feelings on social media.

Some children hide them within, and we know nothing of what they were feeling until it's too late. Our children should never utter these words, and if they do, we should take them very serious. These are words that say, "I'm hurting" or "I've been hurt".

An even greater danger comes from adults and parents who say they did not know their child was suffering, they never said anything to them, or they say they wish they knew what was going on inside their child.

Are we listening to our children, or simply hearing them only? Are we paying attention to them as they try to navigate through their young lives to adulthood?

As parents we should never be so busy socializing or attempting to be friends that we lose sight of what it means to be parents.

Some parents allow themselves to think that abuse (*often called discipline*) is a form of love, and some even dare to call what they do TOUGH LOVE.

What is it that makes a child feel that they would rather be dead than to continue to live, and what is it that makes a child take their life?

Here is a list of children who committed suicide because they did not feel they could get help to deal with bullying in their lives.

Kelly Yeoman (1984–1997), **age 13**, the victim of continuous bullying, harassment and taunting by other students about her weight. In September 1997 things got worse, when a group of youth reportedly gathered at Kelly's home on several consecutive nights, on each occasion throwing food at the house and shouting taunts at Kelly. This 13-year-old told her family, "She'd had enough and was going to take an overdose." She did. Five young people between thirteen and seventeen were convicted of intentionally harassing Kelly in the months leading up to her death.

Dawn-Marie Wesley (1986–2000), **age 14**, a high school student from Canada who died of suicide by hanging herself due to bullying. Dawn committed suicide after continuous bullying by psychological abuse and verbal threats from three female bullies at her high school. She left a note behind to her family that referred to the bullying to which in part said: "If I try to get help, it will get worse. They are always looking for a new person to beat up, and these are the toughest girls. If I ratted, they would get expelled from school and there would be no stopping them. I love you all so much." She committed suicide by hanging herself with her dog's leash in her bedroom.

Nicola Ann Raphael (1985–2001), **age 15**. She was a high school student who died by suicide by an overdose of Coproxamol due to bullying.

Material requested later for legal action found that the bullying had gone back three years. Nicola Raphael took an overdose in 2001 after being tormented over her gothic appearance, she had complained to teachers about the bullying long before she died. The manuscript shows staff clearly knew Nicola, and her being bullied but did not inform her parents."

Ryan Halligan (1989–2003), **age 13**, committed suicide after allegedly being bullied by his classmates in person as well as online. Ryan was repeatedly sent homophobic instant messages, and was threatened, taunted and insulted. Ryan's case has been cited by legislators in various states proposing legislation to curb what is called cyber-bullying.

Megan Meier (1992–2006), **age 13**, died of suicide by hanging herself three weeks before her fourteenth birthday. A year later, Megan's parents urged an investigation into the matter and Megan's suicide and found her suicide was attributed to cyber-bullying through the social networking site MySpace.

Sladjana Vidovic (1992–2008), **age 16**, from Mentor, Ohio, hanged herself in October 2008 jumping from a window with a sheet around her neck. She and her family were from Bosnia. Her family was from Bosnia and because of her accent and name, other students called her names like "Slutty Jana" and "Slut-Jana-Vagina." It got to a point that she just didn't want to live anymore, and hang herself.

Tyler Long (1992–2009), **age 17**, was a gay student with Asperger syndrome (*a developmental disorder characterized by significant difficulty in social interaction, and nonverbal communication along with restricted, and repetitive patterns of behavior and interests. As a milder autism spectrum disorder (ASD). Although not necessary for diagnosis, physical clumsiness and unusual use of language are common in those who suffer with Asperger and typically last for a person's entire life*). Because of his homosexuality and disability, students stole things from him, spit in his food, and call him names like "gay" and "faggot." Tyler's mother had gone to the school to complain about the bullying, the school responded by saying that **"boys will be boys"** or he just **"took it the wrong way."** Two months into his junior year of high school Tyler strapped a belt around his neck and hanged himself from the top shelf of his bedroom closet.

Ty Smalley (1998-2010), **age 11**, was bullied because he was small for his age. Bullies would stuff him into lockers and shove him into trash cans. They would also call him names like "Shrimp" and "Tiny Tim."

Ty was cornered On May 13, 2010 in the school gym, and a bully started a fight by pushing him. Ty never used to fight back, that was not the case this time, he pushed his attacker away. He and the bully were both sent to the principal's office.

Ty was given a three-day suspension, and his bully given only one day of suspension. After school that day, Ty committed suicide by shooting himself with a .22 caliber pistol.

Audrie Pott (1997–2012), **age 15**, a student attending Saratoga High School, California. She died of suicide by hanging herself on September 12, 2012. She had been sexually assaulted by three teenage boys at a party eight days prior and the pictures of the assault were posted online with accompanying bullying. Audrie's suicide had been compared to a young woman in Canada, Rehtaeh Parsons.

Amanda Todd (1996–2012), **age 15**, A Canadian high school student who died by hanging herself due to school bullying and cyberbullying. She died at her home in Port Coquitlam, British Columbia, Canada.

Prior to her death Amanda had posted a video on YouTube using a series of flash cards to tell her experience of being blackmailed into exposing her breasts via webcam, bullied; and physically assaulted.

The video went viral after her death, resulted in international media attention concerning cyber bullying.

Jadin Bell (1997–2013), **age 15**, was an Oregon youth known for his suicide which raised the national profile on youth bullying and gay victimization in bullying. Bell, a 15-year-old gay youth, was allegedly intensely bullied both in person and on the internet because he was gay.

Jadin was a member of the La Grande High School cheer leading team in La Grande, Oregon, where he was a sophomore. On January 14, 2013, Bell went to a local elementary school and hanged himself from the play structure, he did not immediately die from the strangulation and was rushed to the emergency room, where he was kept on life support but later died.

Rehtaeh Parsons (1995–2013), **age 17**, a High School student, who unsuccessfully attempted suicide by hanging herself on April 4, 2013, at her home in Dartmouth, Nova Scotia, Canada, which led to her being in a coma and the decision to switch her life support machine off at Queen Elizabeth II Health Sciences Centre on April 7, 2013.

Rehtaeh death had been attributed to online distribution of photos of an alleged gang rape that occurred 17 months previous to her suicide.

Katelyn Nicole Davis (2004–2016), **age 12**, from Cedartown, Georgia, hanged herself from a tree in her front yard while live streaming the event to Live.me.

The video was broadly shared on social media, particularly on Facebook. Katelyn was an active blogger on multiple social media sites, and recorded dozens of videos leading up to the last month of her life. Katelyn was said to have suffered from depression, and also being bullied at school. She also claimed to be neglected by her biological father, and physically and sexually abused by her stepfather.

Gabriel Taye (2009-2017), **age 8** a third grader From Cincinnati, Ohio. Gabriel was a student at Carson Elementary School where video showed him being knocked unconscious by another child after extending his hand in what appears to be a friendly gesture. Gabriel was kicked by other students for about 5 minutes as he lay unconscious on the floor. Officials reportedly didn't tell Gabriel's mother that he was assaulted, or that he was rendered unconscious. Two days later, the unthinkable happened.

Shortly after arriving home from school at 5:30 p.m. on January 26, the 8-year old hung himself in his bedroom. He was found dead; he had used a knotted necktie to commit suicide from his bunk bed.

As we have already discussed and demonstrated that as parents, adults, and educators, many of us fumbled the ball of parenting at the expense of our children.

Children are life's most precious cargo, but many see them as bothersome, as they interfere with the parent's life, and for some adults these children altered and interrupted their life's and lifestyle.

Hearing does not mean listening

Many parents are not listening to their children as they cry out to them, because they don't see what the child is experiencing is a real problem, or it will just go away, if they socialize more or use some other distraction to help them, and because of this their children turn inward and many hurt themselves even attempting to kill themselves.

What is it that leads a child to want to take their own lives when they have not even truly lived life yet?

Missing the warning signs does not mean they are not there.

There are a number of signs that can contribute to this thinking, a few of which we list here.

1) Not feeling they belong
2) Feelings of neglect/ isolation
3) Low Self-Esteem
4) Physical, emotional, sexual abuse
5) Bullying
6) Change of sleep habits
7) Physical appearance

Why would a child wish themselves dead when they have not experienced life yet?

Domestic violence and bullying are learned behaviors

We are not born bullies, or violent, but can become so, and the more we are exposed to violence and bullying, or see it as the means to achieve goals in our lives, this can begin the process, and encouraged at an early age.

Many adults attempt to have children act and respond as if they are also adults, and will badger (*bully*) the child if they do not act accordingly.

Many adults seek to mentally and emotionally force a child into believing they should feel as the adult instructs and tell them to, removing that child's ability to be an individual thinker, and compassionate or as some would say, showing sportsmanship conduct.

It becomes easy for a parent to decide what career path their child should take, and have no problem with letting that child know how disappointed they would be if they decided to go another direction with their life, and therefore placing unnecessary guilt on that child.

There are many children that suffer from abuse. Some have grown up to have very successful lives. But they still carry with them the wounds and scars of abuse internally.

When a child says they wish they were dead it should be taken very seriously. The children listed here were just that, children. Each of them felt they had no other choice but to end their lives. Lives they never would enjoy.

Let's stop just hearing our children and start listening to them.

These children lost their lives because they did not feel they could talk to the adults in their lives. What kind of images are we giving our children that they don't feel comfortable with coming to us, and that they believe the only course of action for them is to take their young lives?

NOTES

Chapter 8
Being Me

No one knows what's in the mind of a child. What they think, how they feel, or even what they will choose to become when old enough to decide for themselves.

We discover what children want by their actions and their actions are often influenced by their limited experiences.

Many parents however take this selection process away from the child. There are some parents who believe the path they chose, is the one their children should also choose.

Often we rob our children of their identities because many of us want to see our children as smarter, better, and more successful than other children or ourselves and so, we push, punch and drag them into becoming what we want them to be, never allowing them to be themselves or choose for themselves what they would like to do in life.

It's possible for a child to choose the same career path of their parents, but it should not be expected of them or forced on them.

As we've already shown, parents can also be

bully's and the harm that can be done can last a lifetime.

As we have discussed in the previous two books (*In the Ring with heels on, She's the Boss*), people are not property and should never be treated as such.

If you want to know what is going on in the mind of someone, the best way to find out is to ask, not assume.

One of the biggest problems we face is this, many of us as adults don't want to know what someone else thinks or even feel. We believe our thoughts are more important than others, and what we think, is best, especially as it pertains to our children.

Children are not miniature adults, but they are special lives, and the seeds we plant in their consciousness will grow negatively or positively.

I've spoken to adults who as children said, all they wanted to do is be a child and have fun like other children and play games before they became too old to do so.

Many of us have said to our children, "you better enjoy life now; it's not going to always be like that".

Children are explorers and quite naturally see the world differently from adults, and as adults it's our responsibility to keep our children as safe as possible while allowing them to be themselves.

Being me does not mean a "mini-me"

As adults we can have the answers to many questions but that does not mean we have the answers to all questions.

Having children means taking the time to teach and monitor them as well as learn from them.

What are our children doing, what are they avoiding, or should avoid, what do they like, what are they listening to, what are they wearing, or want to wear? These questions are good indicators of their growing personalities and individualization.

Be very mindful that the greatest influences come from the home first. Love, comfort and security are first experienced at home (or should be).

A child will experience balance the moment there is interaction with others outside the home. A parent is to maintain giving their child the right balance to help them make the best decision as they choose a life direction.

It can be a good thing when our children grow up and begin to sound like us to a certain degree. I have been charged on a number of occasions of sounding like my mother, as some of the things she taught us as children had found their way into my life conversations.

As adults, part of our responsibility is to guide our children as they grow and help them discover themselves in the process, and what path they might choose for themselves.

Does this mean we have to agree with their choices, absolutely not, but they should be allowed to make them when mature enough to do so, our mission is to help them see if that choice would be the best for them (*not us*), and understanding the consequences that might accompany their decision. It's also our mission to help them, not choose for them, as life will offer them choices that at times will require great consideration.

Let's not cloud the issue by saying we only want what's best for our children when in fact, we want what's best for us through our children.

This process of decision making can become a case of bullying by strong influence and alienation if rejected by that child.

Just let me be me. If you have no idea what that means, it's time you found out, but in order to do that, you must be willing to do so by opening your ears and closing your mouth.

Being me does not mean our children must follow in our footsteps, by becoming a doctor, a lawyer, or engineer. It means they have our support and encouragement to discover simply who they are.

Theirs a very good book in the market I highly recommend, its title, **"Do what you love the money will follow"** by Marsha Sinetar. It's an amazing book on what it means to actually learn what it means to be "You". It also opens up to the reality that many of us have been caught up in trying to fulfill other people's dreams for us and not our own.

Many of us have become cookie cutter copies of other people and have no real sense of identity or purpose, why? Because we have been programmed to believe certain things can only be done in a certain way.

If that were true many of the inventions and discoveries we enjoy would not exist, from the traffic light to the flashlight.

Creativity is strongest when it is not impeded or obstructed but is allowed to blossom.

One of the greatest expectations should be that our children are not simply our replacements, and that they are allowed to dream, as well as follow their own dreams.

Being me means just that. It's not forcing a child to become what they might not be willing to become, just because we believe we know what's best for them.

When anyone is forced to become what others want them to be, they are faced with thoughts of rebellion, resentment, anger and even violence.

Part of being an adult is being responsible, this does not mean bullying and intimidating to get our way. Our way does not mean it's the best or only way. We must help our children learn to become themselves.

NOTES:

Conclusion

Wake up everybody, it's time to get your heads out of the sand and see what's going on around you.

It's time you understand that Pandora's box has been opened and we will not easily close it.

And now the most precious of cargo is being corrupted and little is being done about it.

We live in a reactive, and not proactive world, and no longer forward thinkers, and as such, violence, and bullying has now taken hold of our country and our children. The innocence is being removed one child at a time.

Bullying is not new, but has been given a new platform through social media and other technology.

We cannot stop social or any other media from existing, but we can do a better job of educating our children concerning their use.

Adversity is the name of bullies, and they seek targets to intimidate, but there are ways to deal with bullies, and that is, get to know what makes them tick. We cannot cure what we refuse to diagnose as a problem.

Now is the time to examine the thoughts, our thoughts before the actions, to review the life leading up to the act. Bullying like so many other issues is preventable. So, the question becomes, what are we, you, going to do about it?

About the Author

Timothy White Sr. has impacted thousands of people throughout the world as an author, teacher, motivational speaker and minister. Mr. White is on a mission to positively influence millions of people through his work, ministry and writing, which currently exceeds 80+ books covering a plethora of topics including bullying, domestic violence, self-help, history and spirituality.

The Cleveland, Ohio native, a father of five, has overcome many adversities in his life including homelessness and losing his beloved wife to cancer in 1994. Through much heartache and disappointments he discovered a new purpose and passion to use writing as a tool to "plant positive seeds."

Mr. White has developed profound spiritual insight into relationships over the years. Mr. White has written multiple books on the topic of abuse including, *In the Ring with Heels On, She's the Boss and Victims of Bullies*. Mr. White writes about these and other issues because of the relevance, and prevalence of domestic and other violence. He believes that, **"Information plus application equals transformation."**

Mr. White is an Evangelist and former pastor. He believes, "God chooses who He uses." He writes, speaks, and ministers to local, national, and international audiences. With an additional 15 new books in the works, Mr. White hopes to give people plenty of "spiritual food" to eat.

White is one of the producers of the documentary *"Where's Gina?"* about missing children on which he was also narrator.

He is a co-developer of a tech company (Gsys LLC) that brought blindside technology to vehicles that made billions for the industry, saving countless lives. He is currently co-hosting a radio show,

*"**Healing the Hurt**"* on WERE 1490am in Cleveland, Ohio on Thursday evenings 8-10 pm with Host, Rev. Brenda Ware-Abrams.

He is currently on the Advisory Board and is a volunteer instructor at the Juvenile Correction centers in Warrensville Heights and Cleveland, Ohio where his book *Seven Signs of Success* is being taught. His book *Victims of Bullies* is, currently, in the City of Cleveland School system to help stop and make aware of solutions to the issue of bullying.

timwhite55@gmail.com   Timwhitepublishing.com

www.ingramcontent.com/pod-product-compliance
Lightning Source LLC
Chambersburg PA
CBHW031222090426
42740CB00007B/674